Giovanna Magi

ALL AVIGNON

104 Photographs in colour

BONECHI

© Copyright 1988
by CASA EDITRICE BONECHI
FIRENZE - via Cairoli 18/b

Diffusion: OVET

13, rue des Nanettes
75011 PARIS
Phone: 43 38 56 80

6, place du Mont Serein
30400 VILLENEUVE-LÈS-AVIGNON
Phone: 90 25 28 63

Printed in E.E.C. by
Centro Stampa Editoriale Bonechi

ISBN 88-7009-107-4

Photo credits
Photographs from the archives of Casa Editrice Bonechi by
LUIGI DI GIOVINE

INDEX

HISTORY

he site of what we call Avignon today has been in-
abited for millennia. About 2000 years ago the Ca-
ares settled the area in the vicinity of a huge cliff
verhanging the Rhône River. These rough soldiers
nd fishermen called their settlement Auoenion,
eaning «lord of the waters» from two Celtic words,
aouen» (whirlpool) and «ion» (lord). When the
ocenses founded Massalia, present-day Marseille, six
undred years before the birth of Christ, they were
mediately attracted by Aouenion's superb geo-
aphical position and dredged a port, later enlarged
y the Romans, in the river. Throughout the Roman
ra, the city, known to the Romans as Avenius, was
a important reference point for all the people
aveling up and down the river for economic or
ommercial reasons. Nevertheless, few vestiges of
oman times are extant today: ruins of a theater,
aces of an archway over some arcading, a few
locks of stone from a triumphal arch are all. This is
ue to the fact that Avignon's magnificent location
ade her constant prey to attack and time and time
gain she was brought under foreign dominion.
onquered first by the Saracens, and then by the
ranks, Burgundians, Ostrogoths, and again Franks,
a the 8th century she fell to the Moors who by this
me were masters of the whole Iberian peninsula.
he Moorish occupation lasted from 734 to 737, the
ear of Charles the Hammer's intervention. The siege
e town was put to in 737 was memorable, and it
as then that most of the Roman monuments met
eir destruction. So much blood was shed in the ter-
ble struggle that a still extant city street was named
d (Rue Rouge) to describe it.
he centuries following the siege were not particularly
oteworthy as far as Avignon history was concerned,
nd it looked as though the city would never come
ut of its anonymity. Then in 1309 a truly outstand-
g event took place—the Papal Court was moved
om Rome to Avignon—and the course of the city's
istory took a new, more exciting, turn. What hap-
ened was that constant bickering among various
actions had made it impossible for the popes to reign
a the Eternal City. Following the brief pontificate of
enedict XI who died in 1304, the Archbishop of
ordeaux, Bertrand de Got, was elected pope and he
ook the name Clement V. One of his staunchest sup-

porters was Philip the Fair, King of France, who had
wielded his influence to have de Got elected with an
eye toward benefiting the French throne. The newly-
elected pope refused to go to Rome for his coronation
and as a result the ceremony was held in Lyon. As
his official residence, Clement V chose Venaissin, a
territory that Raymond, Count of Toulouse, had
ceded to the Church after the Crusades of the Albigenses.
Clement V's successor, John XXII, wanted a more
fitting seat for the Throne of St. Peter, and left the
countryside to set up the papal court at Avignon
which at the time belonged to Provence and was thus
under the dominion of the Anjou. In 1348 Clement
VI purchased the town from Queen Giovanna I of
Sicily for 80,000 florins, and the papal court finally
had a seat of its own.
Nevertheless, even though the territory was not directly under the French crown, the papacy could
hardly fail to be influenced by it.
Thus began the period that has come down in history
as the Avignon Captivity, or the Babylonian Captivity,
as it came to be known from the title Martin Luther's
second pamphlet issued in 1520.
Seven popes, all French reigned at Avignon. Under
their papacies, the city was fortified with great bas-
tions and an immense castle, also fortified, was
erected as the papal residence. The court at Avignon
became one of the most magnificent recorded in
medieval Europe, but this did not mean that all went
smoothly in the new center of Christendom. The spirit
of tolerance that prevailed meant that neither Jews
nor non-Christians were persecuted—in fact, the
former simply paid a special tax to be left in peace—
but it also meant that common criminals, adventur-
ers, counterfeiters, and smugglers who had success-
fully escaped justice in their homelands could do the
same thing in Avignon. Periodically, too, the region
was struck by plagues which caused numerous vic-
tims and it was often prey to another great scrouge of
the Middle Ages, armed bands of soldiers of fortune.
These individuals, half bandits and half soldiers, once
part of the royal armies, roamed the countryside steal-
ing, looting, burning, torturing, and killing. The
popes sought to solve the problem by paying them off
in proportion to their numbers and blessing them.

Then, if this were not enough, the influence of the king of France on the pope became so great that it could be termed actual interference. This resulted in the growing up of a movement clammering for the pope to return to Rome, his natural seat. Petrarch, one of the regulars of the papal court, was also one of the staunchest supporters of the return-to-Rome movement. St. Catherine of Siena exhorted Gregory XI time and time again with loving words («... my sweet father...») to leave the city. St. Bridget of Sweden was another of those who expressed the wishes of practically all of Christendom hoping the pope would decide to move back to Rome.

In 1367 Urban V finally made up his mind to make the move, but the pressure exerted by the French king made him rush back to Avignon and it was his successor, Gregory XI, who made the definitive move in 1377. But the consequences were not what the Catholic world had expected. Following Gregory's death, the Conclave of 1378 elected Bartolomeo Prignano, Archbishop of Bari, who took the name Urban VI. Right away, the French cardinals, highly dissatisfied, held a meeting at Fondi and declared the election of Urban VI null and void and elected another pope, Robert of Geneva, who took the name Clement VII and set up his court in Avignon. This was the anti-pope, the beginning of the division of the Christian world into two parts: the Great Schism of the West had started.

Reciprocally excommunicated, the pope and anti-pope went all out to defeat each other. After long, drawn-out vicissitudes (in which there was even a third pretender to the papal throne, Alexander V), and complicated bargaining and negotiations, the Council of Constance was held in 1414. At this time, both contenders renounced their claims and Martin V was elected pope. Finally a solution to the split that had so painfully lacerated the Church was in sight.

Thereafter, up until the time of the French Revolution, Avignon was administered by a pontifical legate and throughout these centuries the city flourished and was embellished with churches, monuments, and hôtels. Only two major events marked this otherwise uneventful period. The first, terrible, was the plague of 1721 which was survived by only a quarter of the city's 24,000 inhabitants and the second, which took place in 1791, was the annexation of Avignon and Venaissin to France.

Nighttime view of the Palace of the Popes.

THE PALAIS DES PAPES (PALACE OF THE POPES)

The palace took approximately thirty years to build under the reigns of three popes (Benedict XII, Clement VI, and Innocent VI). One of the largest in existence, it covers 15,000 square meters of surface area. From the outside it looks like a fortress with its high walls pierced here and there by narrow openings, massive pointed arches rhythmically punctuating the whole, and huge machicolations which made the castle prac-

tically unconquerable; the interior, on the other hand, full of wall decorations, frescoes, and tapestries has the appearance of a real palace. One can imagine how it must have looked at the time of the papal court of Avignon when the halls were crowded with theologians, princes, kings, cardinals, clergymen and courtiers, not to mention the Italian and French artists. It is true that Petrarch denounced its corruption, but nevertheless Avignon was still the papal court experiencing and living the dawn of the Renaissance. The architects called in to supervise its construction were all Frenchmen, starting from the first summoned by Benedict XII, Mas-

ter Pierre Poisson, who was followed by Jean de Louvres (who worked under Clement VI), while the painters commissioned to decorate it were all Italians, including the Sienese painter Giovanni Luca and Matteo Giovannetti from Viterbo dubbed the «Pope's painter». Simone Martini worked in Avignon from 1339 to 1344, but not in the Palace of the Popes. The whole architectural complex is formed by the union of two buildings: the so-called Old Palace built by Benedict XII between 1334 and 1342 and the so-called New Palace erected under Clement VI between 1342 and 1352 (it was under Clement that the project was completed). It would be hard to find other buildings which so perfectly reflect the character and spirit of their commissioners. The Old Palace, so sober as to be austere, mirrors the austerity of the monastic temperament of Benedict XII (despite the fact that he is said to have kept forty trunks filled to the brim with gold artifacts, jewels, gem stones, and 600,000 florins in the room of Tour Saint-Jean known as the Treasure Hall), whereas the New Palace is the image of Clement VI, lover of art and the courtly life, whose propensity was for luxury and embellishment. The interiors too reflect the characteristics of the different epochs they were built in and the very different, practically opposite, personalities of the two popes they were designed for: Benedict's rooms are more Romanesque, while Clement's are more Gothic. Unfortunately, the interiors underwent transformations throughout the centuries. During the French Revolution, for example, the furniture was destroyed or dispersed and much of the sculpture was set afire. Turned into a barracks in 1810, it received further desecration as many of the frescoes were detached and sold, mutilated and in pieces, to the antique dealers of Avignon. However, the future of the Palace of the Popes now looks as though it will take a rather different turn. In 1969 the city set about restoring the two main wings of the palace as a modern convention hall,

leaving the exceptional beauty of the architecture intact, while at the same time equipping it with the most uptodate and sophisticated fittings available.

Every year in July the spectacles of the Festival of Avignon are held in the huge courtyard in front of the palace. The festival was created in 1947 by Jean Vilar who was also its first director. Here in Avignon Vilar gave life to his most important conceptions of theater even before he founded the T.N.P. (Théâtre National Populaire).

THE PORTE
DES CHAMPEAUX

The main façade of the Palais des Papes (the entrance side) is marked by an elegant five-sided tower on the corner and two graceful defense towers with hook-like spires over the entrance. Toppled during Louis XV's siege of Avignon of 1770, the towers were reconstructed according to rare iconographic documentation in 1933.

Actually named Portes des Saints Pierre et Paul, the entrance portal is better known as Porte des Champeaux. This comes from Rue des Champeaux, originally «Carreria de Champellis» (from the Latin «campelli», little fields), the name given to one of the narrow little streets which, along with gardens, was in the vicinity of the houses standing by the west side of the palace up to the year 1404). Above the entranceway is the coat of arms of Pope Clement VI: a blue stripe and red roses on a silver ground.

The two towers flanking the entranceway.

The façade of the palace with the Porte des Champeaux

THE HALL
OF THE CONSISTORY

This huge hall (119 feet long, 162.5 feet wide, and 32.5 feet high) is one of the most significant in the whole palace. Nowadays the Consistory no longer has the great importance it had in the 14th century when it was the supreme council and supreme court of all of Christendom. Here in this hall, with great pomp and magnificence, the cardinals filed in from a tiny door in the south wall when summoned by the pope. In this hall the pope received kings and ambassadors, here he pronounced the names of those who would enter the Sacred College, here the proceedings for the canonization of Bridget of Sweden were initiated, here Cola di Rienzo was tried and condemned (he was imprisoned for over a year in the Tour de Trouillas). Here Giovanna, Queen of Naples, escaped being condemned (as she failed to appear) for being an accomplice in the murder of her first husband, Andrew of Hungary. Nevertheless, the queen was received in the same hall by Clement VI who authorized her marriage to her cousin, Luigi of Taranto. In fact, is was during her stay in the city that Giovanna, finding herself in urgent need of money, sold Avignon to the pope.

We know that the walls, today hung with Gobelins tapestries, were once covered with frescoes by Matteo Giovannetti who had depicted *figures of saints around God the Father* and a *Coronation of the Virgin with four popes*, possibly the first four who sat on the papal throne of Avignon. Unfortunately, the fire which in 1413 destroyed the whole Consistory wing did not spare the frescoes painted by the master from Viterbo. The hall thereafter came to be known as the «Salle Brûlé» (burnt room and in fact the curious rosy hue that the stone of the east wall still bears today recalls the famous fire of five centuries ago.

On the far side of the hall are two fine *wooden statues*, unfortunately in rather poor condition, and three cabinet panels from the Tour de la Livrée d'Albane. Above are nine paintings with *portraits* of popes.

General view of the
Hall of the Consistory.

Detail of a wooden statue. ▶

The far side of the
Hall of the Consistory.

Chapelle Saint-Jean

South wall: Calling of Sts. James and John; Vision of St. John at Patmos; St. John and the resurrection of Drusiana.

Chapelle Saint-Jean

West wall: Crucifixion; Christ entrusting His Mother to St. John.

**Chapelle
Saint-Jean**

North wall:
Baptism of
Christ; John the
Baptist being
interrogated by
the Levites,
Banquet of
Herod,
Beheading of St.
John.

**Chapelle
Saint-Jean**

East wall: Birth
of St. John the
Baptist, Sacrifice
of Zacheriah and
apparition of the
Angel Gabriel.

THE GRAND TINEL

Overlying the Hall of the Consistory is the «magnum tinellum,» one of the largest rooms in the palace (it measures 155.5 × 32.5 feet). The hall has six huge vaulted windows overlooking the garden, surmounted by five smaller ones. Originally the ceiling was decorated with gold stars against a blue ground, but the great fire of 1413 which destroyed the frescoes in the Hall of the Consistory also destroyed this one, as well as those decorating the walls painted by Matteo Giovannetti in 1345.

The pope's meals were prepared and kept hot in the fireplace rebuilt against the north side of the room. The pontiff dined at a table set up along the south wall, while his guests were seated at tables along the side walls. The deliberations and secret balloting of the cardinals took place in a tiny oratory off the Grand Tinel on the east side. A passageway from an outside balcony led to the upper kitchen.

THE UPPER KITCHEN

Clement VI's great square kitchen covered by pyramidal vaulting is one of the most unusual rooms in the palace. Its outstanding feature is a soaring chimney shaped like an upside down funnel which can be seen from a great distance and which is one of the building's oddities. The shape of the kitchen and its monumentality reiterate the fortress-like aspect of the palace, even though history tells us that once, during the siege of 1398, a contingent of enemy soldiers commanded by a certain Geoffroy de Boucicaut managed to gain en-

trance by way of the kitchen drain pipes. Luckily, the noise made by a ladder falling attracted the attention of the inhabitants and the invaders were taken prisoner.

THE CHAPELLE SAINT-MARTIAL

Located on the second floor of the Tour Saint-Jean, this tiny oratory (19.5′ × 17′) owes its name to the fresco cycle by Matteo Giovannetti depicting scenes from the *life of St. Martial*, apostle and patron of Limoges, who, according to legend, was a contemporary of Christ. Undoubtedly, the subject matter was selected because Pope Clement VI who commissioned the cycle was a native of Limoges. Painted in 1344-1345, the story begins on the ceiling, continues on the upper register, and ends on the lower one. Each scene is explained by a Latin inscription. Around the walls below the two registers runs a mock marble base surmounted by Gothic arches. The *altarpiece* is said to have been painted by Giovannetti himself. The story recounts the life of the saint with various episodes of his youth, his mission in Gaul, the miracles he performed in Tulle and Limoges, and his death which is illustrated on the east side of the lower register in the scene showing his soul borne by two angels being welcomed to the heavenly realm.

The frescoes bear witness to the exceptional skill in portraiture of the painter, who, like his contemporary Simone Martini, greatly in-

fluenced 14th century French painting, although they also sport the elegant line typical of the International Style which was the dominant school of the period.

Above:
detail of the frescoes
of the Chapelle St.-Martial.

Below:
A Gothic window breaks up the painted decoration of the Chapelle St.-Martial.

THE ANTECHAMBER

This room, also known as the Pope's Antechamber, was where people granted special audiences with the pope waited to be received.

Originally decorated with fescoes of which only traces are now extant, the room is hung with five huge *tapestries reproducing Raphael's famous frescoes in the Stanze of the Vatican.* The ceiling was once made of wood and the flooring, like the others in the palace, was originally of terracotta tiles whose design has not come down to us.

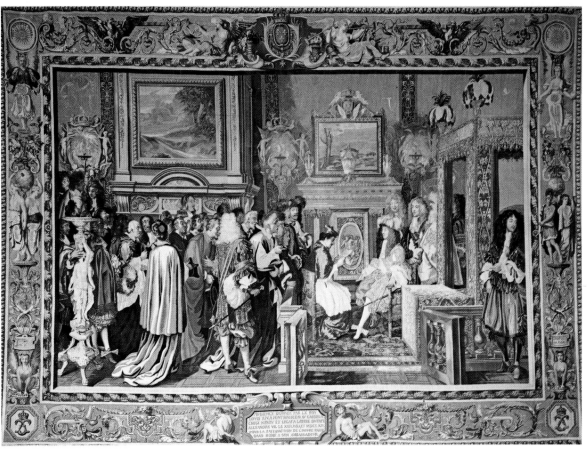

19

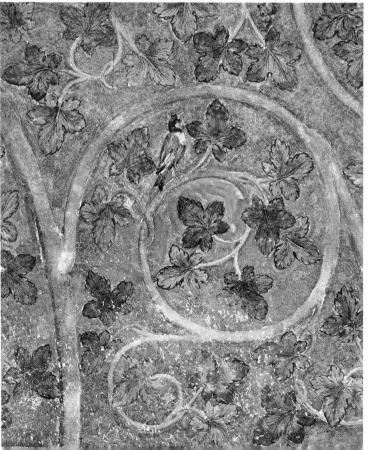

THE POPE'S BEDCHAMBER

Located in the center of the massive Tour du Pape, also known as the Great Tower, the bedchamber is a square-shaped room, approximately 32.5′ per side, with a corner fireplace and two windows. It is likely that when Clement VI took possession of the room he found it too austere for his taste and had the wall decoration changed. The walls, in fact, are adorned with a bright and elaborate fresco cycle depicting birds flying amidst grape-vines and squirrels scampering up and down oak bowers. The frescoes were executed in tempera directly on the stone walls. Recently, using the authentic tile flooring discovered in 1963 beneath the «studium» of Benedict XII, the flooring of this room was re-covered with painted tiles imitating the 14th century originals.

Detail of the wall decoration.

Fresco showing the *piscarium*.

THE DEER ROOM

Located on the fourth floor of the Tour de la Garde-Robe, this is a tiny square-shaped room whose appearance is much brighter and gayer than the other rooms we have seen up to now. In fact, whereas the preceding rooms are all decorated with religious scenes and sacred subjects, this room is frescoed with a profane subject, one which was very much in fashion during that period: the hunt. All kinds of hunting are illustrated, ranging from hunts with falcons to hunts with dogs, but the room's name comes from the scene on the west wall showing a deerhound as he sinks his teeth into the prey, a deer. Falcon-hunting, on the east wall, shows a figure in the typical pose of the falconer with the bird perched on his outstretched right hand. The scene on the north wall depicts fishing with four figures around a pool, most likely a depic-

Detail of a fresco.

The painted ceiling.

tion of the «piscarium» which once existed in Avignon. This was a kind of artificial lake into which fish that had been caught elsewhere were thrown before being served up as part of the pope's sumptuous banquets.

The name of the painter who frescoed the room in 1343 has not come down to us, although the style seems to have been clearly inspired by the Franco-Flemish tapestries illustrating hunting scenes. At first, a tentative attribution was made to Robin de Romans, active at the court at the time, who was undoubtedly only a minor figure among all the great masters then working under the popes. According to a new theory, the subject, elegance, and originality are French, whereas the skillful use of perspective and the modeling of the figures are definitely Italian, so that Matteo Giovannetti, who was one of the foremost artists of the day as Clement VI's official court painter, has been attributed with the supervision of the whole project.

Detail of the falcon hunt.

Scene of the hunt with a ferret.

General view of the North Sacristy and, in the two photos below, the statues of the Duke of Burgundy and the Emperor Charles IV.

THE NORTH SACRISTY

The North Sacristy, also known as the Pope's Sacristy, is reached by way of the Grande Chapelle. Irregularly shaped with a pointed arch ceiling, it is full of *casts of statues of kings and cardinals*. In the eastern bay is the end of the so-called «Pont du Innocent VI» which Pope Innocent had built in 1360 to join the Petit Tinel to the Grande Chapelle.

THE GRANDE CHAPELLE

This imposing hall, 169 feet long, was originally called the «New Chapel,» although it is now known as the «Clementine Chapel» as it was Pope Clement VI's private chapel. The architecture, in the finest southern French Gothic style, features seven bays covered by ribbed vaulting and four huge windows on the south side set off by fluted pilasters joined to the ribs of the vaults. The bare and unadorn walls we see today were once hung with tapestries on ceremonial days. On one side of the hall is a reconstruction of the *altar* on which Clement VI celebrated the All Saints' Mass of 1352. All that has come down to us of this historic altar is a part of the monolithic base which still bears the consecration cross carved on the edge and, in the middle, a cavity which was filled with relics during religious ceremonies.

The Grande Chapelle, or Clementine Chapel.

The South Sacristy.

THE SOUTH SACRISTY

The South Sacristy, reached by way of a vaulted passageway in the Grande Chapelle, is located in the Tour Saint-Laurent. It is also known as the «Vestment Room» since it was here that the pope changed into his elaborate robes for the ceremonies. Recently, *casts of the tombs* of various popes, including those of Clement V, the first pope of Avignon, Clement VI, Innocent VI, and Urban V, have been set up here.

On the following pages

Fenêtre de l'Indulgence. The pope bestowed his triple blessing on the crowd assembled in the Place du Palais from this window (although the one we see today is a 20th century replica of the original). Also, this is where the pope received the «triregnum» (papal tiara) on his coronation day.
Porte de la Grande Chapelle. The portal leading into the Grande Chapelle still preserves its original beauty, mostly a result of the superb sculptural decoration. In the architrave are remains of a Last Judgment and, along the walls, fantastic animals, bearded heads, and grotesque designs.

The Palace of the Popes - Salle de la Grande Audience: ceiling fresco by Matteo Giovannetti.

THE SALLE DE LA GRANDE AUDIENCE

Located on the ground floor of the Palais Neuf is the Great Audience Hall measuring an impressive 169 × 51.4 feet and almost 36 feet in height. Masterpiece of Jean de Louvres, it is divided into two parts by a row of composite columns which are joined to the ribs of the vaulting. Along the walls just beneath the ribs are carved capitals whose animal figures were sculpted by highly skilled, albeit anonymous, artists. Twenty *figures of prophets* and Old Testament figures executed by Matteo Giovannetti for 600 golden florins

in 1352-1353 adorn the star-studded blue ceiling. Each of the figures is wearing a phylactery (a parchment strip used by the Jews) bearing inscriptions from their Books. Unlike the ceiling frescoes which have come down to us beautifully preserved, the fresco on the north wall was totally destroyed in 1822. Nevertheless, on the basis of a description published three years before their destruction, we know that the subject depicted was a five-register *Last Judgment* peopled with a host of popes, bishops, and clergymen. Between the two east windows are barely visible traces of a *Crucifixion* which are nevertheless sufficient to reveal the unmistakable style of Giovannetti, especially in the delicate treatment of the figure

of the Virgin.
This hall was also called the «Room of the Great Suits». In fact, in a special zone, separated from the rest of the room by a partition sat the thirteen ecclesiastical judges who made up the Court of the Holy Roman Rota, otherwise known as the Sacra Rota. The origin of the name is not certain-it might have come from the circular seating arrangement of the judges (these were appointed by the pope and were presided over by a deacon, the «primus inter pares»). Another theory attributes it to the custom of having the cases being discussed in turn, and a third to the fact that the codices were kept upon rotating lecterns. Whatever its origin, the Sacra Rota is indeed

very old: its first known rules and regulations date back to 1331 under John XXII. The lawyers involved in the cases and the dignitaries of the papal court were seated around the partition separating the Court from the rest of the room which was reserved for the public who sat along the wall.

THE SALLE DE LA PETITE AUDIENCE

Placed against the «Guardroom», the Salle de la Petite Audience (on the west side of the Grande Audience) was turned into an arsenal in the early 1600s. Originally it was where the so-called «contradictions» (or minor cases) arising during the trials were heard and judged by the Auditeur des Conredits who was seated on a built-in bench on the north side of the hall. The present decorative scheme of the room dates, however, from the period of the transformation. The vaulted ceilings are covered with grisaille frescoes depicting military trophies and standards with Latin inscriptions (*desiderio pacis, terrori hostium, publicae quieti*) and the ribbing is painted to suggest imitation marble. The lower register has mock faceting painted black. In the painting showing the plague that struck the city of Tarascon in 1721, there is a portrait of Monseigneur Gonteri, Archbishop of Avignon, praying for his city to be spared.

THE SALLE DU CONCLAVE

When several rooms of the palace were restructured as a convention center, the Salle du Conclave was made into the auditorium. Covering a surface area of over 400 m² and seating 500, the hall has been equipped with the most sophisticated devices, including slide and movie projectors for super 8 and 16 millimeter film and booths for simultaneous translation in four languages. All of the rooms of the palace are involved in the restructuration project: the Salle de la Grande Audience, for example, will be turned into a social hall for receptions and banquets for up to 800 people.

THE CATHEDRAL

The full name of the cathedral of Avignon is Notre-Dame-des Domes, perhaps from the Latin «domnus», the title given to the clergy.

The origins of the church are quite obscure, although the building is believed to date back to the 4th century, and, according to legend, was founded by St. Martha in honor of the Virgin. It was subsequently rebuilt in the Romanesque style and consecrated in 1069. The church we see today, however, is even later and dates from 1140-1160, although over the centuries it was remodeled time and time again. Abandoned during the French Revolution, it was re-consecrated in 1822. Notre-Dame was the scene of many historical events: here, in 1333, before leaving for the Crusade against the Turks, Philip VI of France, Philip of Navarre, and John of Bohemia received from Pope John XXII the holy cross to protect them in their holy war and here in 1388 Louis II of Anjou, King of Sicily and Jerusalem, was crowned by Clement VII in the presence of Charles VI.

The church is surmounted by a square-shaped bell tower, 127 feet high. It was rebuilt in 1341 after having been toppled during the siege of the Palais des Papes. In 1859 a gilded castiron *statue of the Virgin* was placed on the top. The exterior is adorned with numerous works of art. The haunting *Calvary* on the church yard is a sculptural group executed in 1819 by Baussan. The elegant portico with its fluted columns topped by Corinthian capitals and architrave was clearly influenced by Roman architecture. I was here that Simone Martini, the Sienese master who died in Avignon in 1344, painted the frescoe of the *Virgin surrounded by angels* and *Blessing Christ* which, together with their sinopias, are exhibited in the Palais des Papes.

The Cathedral viewed from its right side. ▶

Detail of Baussan's Calvary. ▶

Interior

The original plan of the building comprised an aisleless interior with a barrel-vaulted ceiling and a dome over the crossing. During the 14th through 16th centuries, a number of side chapels were added. The choir was enlarged in 675 and during the 1600s as well he apse was completely redesigned by Louis-François de la Valfenière who also added the five windows in the center. The simple Romanesque style interior was done over in 1672 and the tribune was erected in the elaborate Baroque style by Pierre Péru.

The nave extends 75 feet and is 28 feet wide and 49 feet tall. Flanking the entrance are *statues of St. Martha* (on the right) and *Mary Magdalene* (left), attributed to Pierre Mignard the Younger which were originally in the monastery of the Celestins. The highlights of the numerous works of art include: the 13th century white marble *Episcopal Throne* with evangelist symbols carved on the sides (the lion for St. Mark and the ox for St. Luke); a moving 16th century painted terracotta *Christ* fraught with reserved sorrow; and a fresco of the *Baptism of Christ with donors* executed in 1422 (in the Chapel of St. John the Baptist). The paintings adorning the other chapels were painted in 1838 by Eugène Devéria. Inside the church are the tombs of 157 cardinals and clergymen, including those of two popes. The supposed *tomb of Benedict XII*, a collection of various elements added to the original group executed by Jean Lavenier between 1342 and 1345, is to be found in the apse. The *tomb of John XXII* is in one of the chapels. As its style and conception are closely related to contemporary tombs of bishops found in the south of England, it has been attributed to Hug Wilfred who is known to have designed the funerary chapel of the same pope.

The Cathedral

The interior with the statues of Sts. Mary Magdalene (left) and Martha (right).

The Cathedral - Interior: the chapel of the Holy Sacrament.

The Cathedral - Interior: the Episcopal Throne

The Cathedral - Interior: painted terracotta sculpture of Christ.

HIC IACET
BENEDICTVS PAPA XII
OBIIT
DIE XXX APRILIS
ANNI MCCCXLII

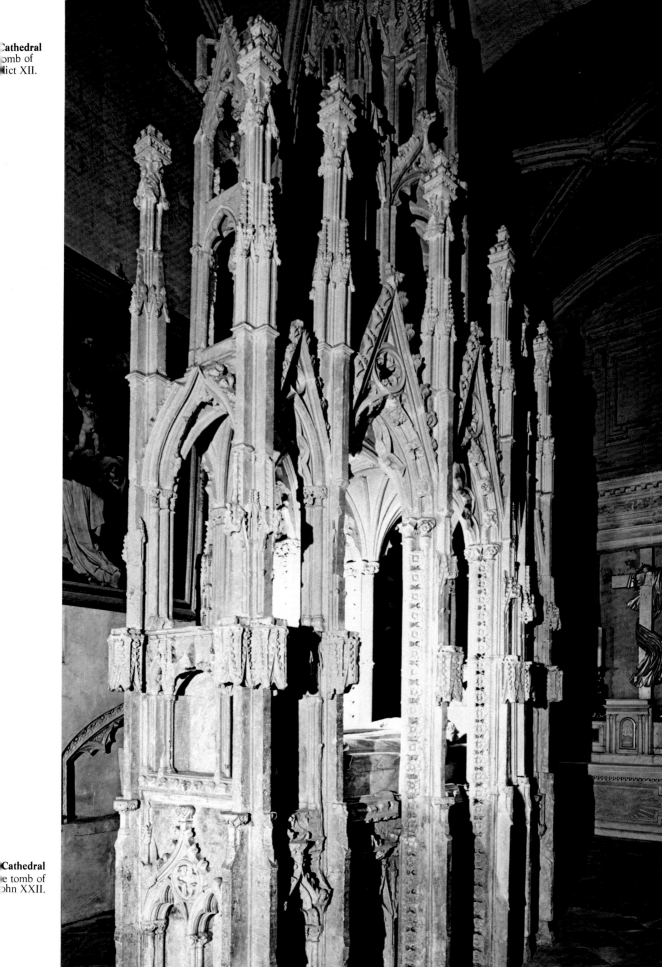

The right side of the Cathedral viewed from the Jardin du Rocher des Doms.

The picturesque train sightseers take to the peak.

The lake in the Jardin du Rocher des Doms.

THE JARDIN DU ROCHER DES DOMS

The Rocher des Doms is probably the most picturesque spot in Avignon. Leaving the cathedral and taking the gently-sloping road to the right which runs alongside the park, all of a sudden we find ourselves immersed in the greenery of the Jardin du Rocher. Here, according to legend, the Emperor Augustus wanted to construct a temple dedicated to the North Wind on this, the highest point of the city. The view that greets our eye is truly breathtaking. All of a sudden the seemingly endless landscape of the Rhône valley lies at our feet. On the opposite side of the riverbanks is the Tower of Philip the Fair, while in the background we can make out the slopes of Mont Ventoux. What was once exposed rock battered by the wind is today a splendid park with charming lakes, statuary, and musk-lined grottos.

A great favorite with sightseers (who reach the peak by means of a charming little train), the Rocher affords the finest view of the delightful countryside surrounding the city that the popes chose as their residence for a brief but splendid period.

THE HÔTEL
DES MONNAIES

Opposite the Palais des Papes is the elaborate Baroque façade of the Hôtel des Monnaies. The building was erected in 1619 to house the papal legation of Cardinal Scipione Borghese whose coat of arms with dragons and eagles is visible on the exterior. Later, the building was turned into a barracks for the cavalry and, during the French Revolution, it was the headquarters for the «gendermerie». Finally, in 1860 it became the Conservatory of Music and it still serves that purpose today.

The contrast between the building's overall austere look, in truth almost military, and the elaborately decorated façade with the dashing eagles along the cornice, is quite striking.

THE PETIT
PALAIS

The building's name comes from the fact that it is much smaller than the nearby Palais des Papes. Erected in 1317, it was remodeled for Cardinal Arnaud de Via, nephew of Pope John XXII. After his death, it was purchased by Benedict XII who made it the official headquarters of the Avignon episcopate. Fortified during the Great Schism, it was later put to siege and bombed. The present appearance of the building dates from the late 1400s. Although its military and defense elements were retained, new touches, befitting the new Renaissance taste, were added: decorative elements and spacious rooms illuminated by windows looking out on the river made it less austere-looking. Major changes were wrought by Cardinal Giuliano della Rovere, later Pope Julius II, who contributed much to the embellishment of the building. Many famous people were guests in the palace, among them Cesare Borgia in 1498 and Francis I in 1533. During Louis XIV's sojourn in Avignon in 1663, Anne of Austria and the Duke of Orleans stayed here. When the state of Avignon was annexed to France, the palace was sold. In 1826 it

The Petit Palais viewed from the outside.

The courtyard of the Petit Palais.

was used as a seminary and in 1905 it was turned into a trade school. Finally, it became a museum, one of the finest specialized museums in France, when the Calvet and Campana collections were united under its roof. Boasting over four hundred 13th-16th century Italian school works, its highlights include the **Virgin and Child** (Room 15), a youthful painting by the 15th century Florentine master Sandro Botticelli. This tiny masterpiece, although still showing traces of the influence of Filippo Lippi, Botticelli's master, already reveals Botticelli's more delicate use of line and his typical tender, almost languid, rendering of faces.

There is also a **Sacra Conversazione** by Vittore Carpaccio. (The Venetian master's signature, *A Victore Carpatio ficti*, is painted on the rock in the lower lefthand corner.) Dated 1515, and thus one of Carpaccio's mature works, this oil panel represents, starting from the left, Sts. Joseph, Anne, John the Baptist, the Virgin and Child, two music-making angels, and Sts. Elizabeth and Zacheriah. In the middle-ground St. Jerome is portrayed on the craggy rock, while a turreted city is shown in the background.

Sandro Botticelli: Virgin and Child.

Vittore Carpaccio: Sacra Conversazione.

43

THE PLACE
DE L'HORLOGE

The picturesque Place de l'Horloge is reached by way of the almost mile-long Rue de la République which runs from the city walls to the Palais des Papes. Now crowded with outdoor cafés which are a favorite meeting-place of the young people of the whole region, the square was once the Roman forum of Avignon. On the square, in addition to the theater, is the Hôtel de Ville, built during the Second Empire. The Hôtel is built around the remains of the Tour de l'Horloge, all that is extant of a Gothic building, the Convent of the Dames de Saint-Laurent. The tower is also known as the Tour

de Jaquemart because on its summit it has a carillon with two figures that strike the hours.

THE CHURCH
OF ST. PIERRE

Destroyed and rebuilt several times, the church was remodeled in the 14th century by Cardinal Pietro da Prato, Bishop of Palestrina and Deacon of the Holy College, who also financed the project. It was consecrated on July 13, 1458.
The most striking element of the building is its elaborate Flamboyant Gothic façade—also bearing traces of the Early Renaissance style as well—which was designed by a native of Avignon, the painter-architect Philippe Garcin, and

erected between 1512 and 1520. The majestic *portal* with its carved doors in the middle of the tower-flanked façade may unreservedly be ranked as one of the finest in Provence. The doors were commissioned by a wealthy merchant of Spanish origin, a certain Michel Lopis, who awarded the project to Antoine Volard, a woodcarver, born in Dauphiné, but resident of Avignon. Volard agreed to do the job for sixty gold écus and he carved the almost 13-foot-high solid walnut doors in 1551. The subjects of the panels are the *Annunciation* on the right and *St. Michael slaying the dragon and St. Jerome with the lion* on the left. In the column dividing the two doors is a sculpture of the *Virgin and Child* surmounted by reliefs of arabesque designs, chimeras, and

St. Pierre

View of the apse and belltower built by Blaise Lécuyer in 1496.

View of the portal.

Portal: detail of the Virgin and Child.

Portal: detail of the lefthand panel with Sts. James and Michael.

Portal: detail of the righthand panel with the Annunciation.

angels holding horns-of plenty and strewing flowers and fruit.

The nave, measuring 83 × 32.5 feet, contains some noteworthy works. The fine late 15th century *pulpit* with six statuettes of prophets and apostles in the niches was carved by an unknown master. Another outstanding work is the Renaissance stone *altar frontal* executed by Imbert Boachon in 1526. The elaborate gilded carvings of the *choir*—in sharp contrast to the simple un- adorn nave— were executed in 1670 by three artists (Laffanant, Trentoul, and Gallois) after a de- sign by François de la Valfrenière. Above the choir stalls are depic- tions of flowers alternating with views of architecture.

St.-Agricol.

The Church of the Pénitents Noirs - The façade.

The portal of the Baroncelli-Javon Palace.

The Church of the Pénitents Noirs - Detail of the façade.

St.-Didier - *Francesco Laurana:* the altar frontal known as Notre Dame du Spasme.

Although the Palais des Papes is the foremost monument in Avignon, there are many other churches and buildings of note in the city. The **church of Saint-Agricol,** mentioned in several texts dating back to the 10th century, is a Gothic building with a Provençal façade erected at the end of the 15th century. The portal at the top of a flight of late 15th century stairs still has its original 15th century Gothic panels with a *statue of the Virgin* in the middle, and an *Annunciation* executed by the Lorrain artist Ferrier Bernard in 1489 on the tympanum. At the end of the nave is the so-called *Doni altar frontal*, a masterpiece of the art of stonecarving executed by Imbert Boachon in 1525.

Not far from here, between the Place de l'Horloge and the Hôtel de la Préfecture, is the **Baroncelli-Javon Palace** which the Florentine banker Pietro Baroncelli had built over the ruins of pre-existing buildings. The palace was considered the most beautiful Gothic mansion in the city. One of the main reasons for its fame was its superb *portal*, executed between 1485 and 1499, and surmounted by a design of entwining mulberry branches. Due to the fact that it stood by the Collège du Roure, the palace came to be known as the Palais du Roure. Today it is a center for studies on Provençal folklore and literature (founded in 1952).

The façade of the **church of the Pénitents Noirs**, designed by Thomas Lainée, is in pure 18th century style. Corinthian style in the lower floor, it becomes Tuscan in the upper one in which the artist depicts a flurry of angels carrying the head of John the Baptist on a platter. This is a reference to the fact that the Confraternity of the Pénitents Noirs was founded in commemoration of the decapitation of the Baptist.

Lastly, we come to the **church of Saint-Didier,** supposedly founded in the 7th century by St. Agricol. Rebuilt as a Gothic church between 1356 and 1459 by Jacques Alasaud and financed thanks to the legacy left by Cardinal Bertrand de Déaux, the church was consecrated on September 20, 1359. The interior is extremely simple and unadorn. In the first righthand chapel is a marble *altar frontal* that King René commissioned in 1478 from the great Italian master, Francesco Laurana. The Calvary depicted upon it is one of the highest expressions of Renaissance art to be found in all of France. Due to the striking rendering of the figures captured in their sorrow and pain amidst a superb setting of Italian architecture, the altar frontal has come to be known as Notre Dame du Spasme. In addition, several interesting frescoes contemporary with the Avignon papacy and attributed to Italian artists were discovered in the chapel containing the baptismal font in 1965.

THE MUSEE CALVET

At number 65 of Rue Joseph Vernet, one of the first streets to be paved in Avignon, is the building erected between 1741 and 1754 by Jean-Baptiste Franque known as the Hôtel Villeneuve-Martignan. A fine *wrought-iron gate* executed by a native of Avignon, Noël Biret, in 1886 leads to the inner courtyard of the building. The garden, with its statuary artfully placed amidst the greenery and strolling peacocks, was described in «Les Mémoires d'un Touriste» by Stendhal who visited it in 1837 and compared its peaceful and quiet setting to those of the finest Italian churches.

The name of the museum comes from that of its founder, Esprit-Claude Calvet, who was a professor of medicine in Avignon and an archeologist and bibliophile as well. When he died on July 25, 1810, he left his huge library, art collections, and funds to create the museum to his native city. Soon other bequests were added to the original one, among which an important collection of Greek marbles left by the Nani family of Venice and the Biret collection of wrought-iron, ranked after Rouen as the finest in France. Comprising both paintings and sculpture, the museum collection covers all the French and Avignon schools from the 14th to 20th centuries. Also on display are numerous works by Joseph Vernet, the painter from Avignon who died in 1789.

Musée Calvet - View of the 14th and 16th century halls.

Musée Calvet - Two wooden sculptures.

Musée Calvet - *Joseph Vernet:* the Tempest.

Musée Calvet - *Joseph Vernet:* the Harbor Entrance.

The Flemish school is represented by the *Hoboken* or *St. George Kermesse.* The painting was once attributed to Pieter Brueghel the Elder, but nowadays art historians are inclined to attribute it to an unknown follower of the great Fleming capable of skillfully imitating his master's favorite subject matter. Outstanding among the 19th century paintings is the *Death of Bara* by Jacques-Louis David who rendered the classical-inspired female nude in the new Romantic fashion.

The museum also features an archeological collection. Noteworthy are the *neolithic tomb* and the famous *stele du Rocher.* The discovery of the stele in the Jardin du Rocher des Doms in 1960, was responsible for completely changing the theories, up to that time universally accepted, regarding the origins of Avignon. Originally, it was thought that the tribes who had settled the area had brought little or no culture of their own, whereas now, after studying the old stone, it is believe that the first inhabitants of Avignon were much more numerous and advanced than had previously been theorized.

Musée Calvet

Unknown Fleming:
the Hoboken Kermesse.

Musée Calvet

Jacques-Louis David:
the Death of Bara.

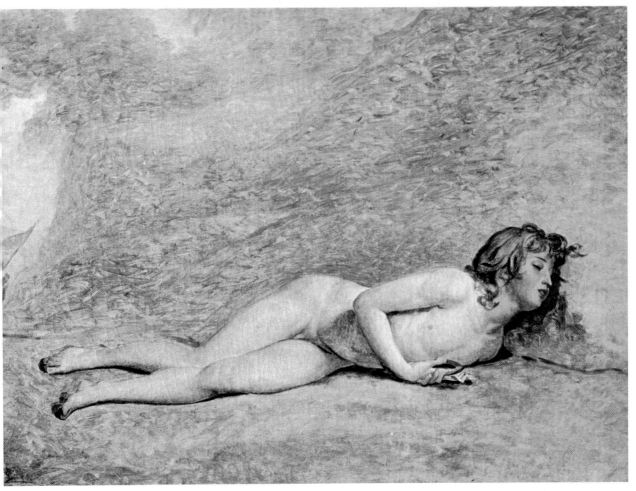

Musée Calvet   Neolithic tomb.

The du Rocher Stele.

THE MONASTERY OF THE CELESTINS

The huge monastery complex of the Celestins was founded in 1393 on the site of the tomb—said to be miraculous—of Cardinal Pierre de Luxembourg of Lorraine, who died at the age of nineteen, here in Avignon. It was commissioned by Cardinal Robert of Geneva (later Pope Clement VII) and King Charles VI. Pierrin Morel, a native of Lorraine, supervised the construction of the church (he is responsible for the apse, the transept, and two bays). The elegant *cloister* dates from the early 1400s. The church has the typical rather squat and, at the same time, imposing appearance of the Northern French Gothic style.

THE REMPARTS (CITY WALLS)

The city walls of Avignon, the famous *Remparts*, would hardly be ranked first-rate by experts in military defensive architecture. They lack a good stretch of machicolation and their towers open up on the city side—in short, they go against all the most advanced defense criteria of the times. Yet such «carelessness» in fortifying the city was not neces-

Detail of the walls of Avignon.

A stretch of Avignon wall.

sarily due to chance, since the popes already possessed what was practically an unconquerable fortress in the Palais des Papes. Hence, the *Remparts* were not an essential, but an added, element in the defense of Avignon. Yet today it would be hard to imagine the cityscape without them and thus they have become an essential element after all, in a way that has nothing to do with defense.

Built between 1356 and 1370, the elliptical-shaped walls with their numerous towers, crenellated glacis, and openings encircle the city for approximately three miles. Originally they had seven portals, but their number was later doubled. Rebuilt at the end of the 15th century by Cardinal della Rovere, they underwent extensive restoration in the 19th century under the supervision of Viollet-le-Duc. During the restoration work, over 4500 curious marks were discovered on the stone blocks. They were later deciphered as symbols to identify the stonecutters engaged in building the walls. As the laborers were paid a certain sum for each stone they produced, the marks meant that every man was able to easily total up his earnings.

During the period of the French Revolution, it was decided that the whole wall should be torn down and the stone blocks sold one by one. Fortunately, as the construction was too solid and would not give way under the blows of the pickaxes, this proved impossible and the project was abandoned once and for all.

THE PONT D'AVIGNON (PONT ST. BENEZET)

This is the bridge immortalized in the celebrated song we all were taught as children. Its history is closely tied in with the charming legend of Saint Bénézet, who, although never canonized, is believed to have really existed.

One day young Bénézet, a shepherd boy who kept his flock near Viviers where he was born, heard a heavenly voice ordering him to go to Avignon and build a bridge over the rushing waters of the Rhône. The boy had never in his life left the hillside, but he se

Pont St.-Bénézet with the Chapelle St.-Nicholas

On these pages:
four views of Pont St.-Bénézet.

off and on his way he met an angel who brought him before the Bishop of Avignon. The bishop had him perform a test which was to lift a rock so heavy that not even thirty grown men would have been able to budge it. Yet Bénézet, fortified by a sudden miraculous strength, effortlessly raised it from the ground and ran to set it by the riverbank. «This», he said, «will be the first stone of the foundation of the bridge». The crowd which had in the meantime gathered was caught up in an incredible enthusiasm and, according to the story, an improvised public collection brought in five thousand gold écus.

Whatever its origins, the bridge as we know it was begun in 1177 and finished in January 1185. Its twenty-two arches spanning 2925 feet of the two branches of the Rhône made up the first bridge that travelers encountered sailing upstream from the sea. Almost completely demolished after the fall of Avignon in 1226, it was partially rebuilt, and then in 1680 completely abandoned. Today only four spans are left.

Also extant is a little chapel, Chapelle Saint-Nicholas, on the second pylon. It is composed of a Romanesque chapel surmounted by a Gothic chapel flanked by a 16th century apse inside of which were once preserved the remains of St. Bénézet (they had been moved here from the church of the Celestins in 1674), but the relics were lost during the tempestuous years of the French Revolution.

Panoramic view of Villeneuve-lès- Avignon with Fort St.-André on the right.

VILLENEUVE-LES-AVIGNON

On the right bank of the Rhône, almost as a counterpart to the city of Avignon, is the medieval town of Villeneuve-lès-Avignon. Its origins date back to the Benedictine monastery of Saint-André founded in the 10th century on the hill which in those days was known as Mont Andaon. At the outset of the Middle Ages it was still an island surrounded by a branch of the Rhône which would later dry up. In 1292 Philip the Fair, well aware of the spot's tremendous strategic importance, decided it was the place to found a new city, the «ville neuve», which would serve, as the stronghold of the Capetin monarchy, to counterbalance Avignon, stronghold first of the Empire and then of the papacy. The river united and divided the two facing cities at the same time. In fact, after the Crusade of the Albigenses, the King of France owner of the river but no farther, made the citizens of Avignon pay a tax when the Rhône overflowed during the rainy season. The arrival of the popes in Avignon was a not−to-be-missed chance for the city to develop. Unable to find residences worthy of their rank in the city, many cardinals moved to the «suburbs», commissioning fifteen or so splendid palaces, the «livrées», in Villeneuve. Prosperity did not abandon the city once the popes had returned to Rome. Only the coming of the French Revolution brought an end to the ecclesiastic and aristocratic wealth that for centuries upon centuries had characterized Villeneuve life. Many vestiges of the city's glorious past are still visible today. Foremost among these is the massive, solitary *Tour de Philippe-le-Bel* at the beginning of the bridge of Saint-Bénézet. The 104-foot tower, built in 1302, is all that remains of a castle which once served to defend the entrance to the bridge. The upper story and watchtower were added in the 14th century. From the top there is a superb view of the «city of the popes» facing the «city of the cardinals». Another splendid view is to be had from the heights of the *Fort Saint-André*, the town built during the second half of the 14th century by John the Good and Charles V. It is entirely enclosed within crenellated walls pierced by

a magnificent defense portal with massive twin towers, built in 1362, on either side. The towers were clearly influenced by Northern military architecture and today represent one of the finest examples of medieval fortification extant.

The sumptuous mansion which once belonged to Cardinal Arnaud de Via was turned into a collegiate church in 1333 and now serves as the parish church. It has an imposing square apse which, before being remodeled between 1344 and 1355, was a massive crenellated tower with pointed mullioned windows. In the sacristy of the aisleless interior there is a tiny masterpiece of ivory carving: a painted *Virgin* sculpted from an elephant tusk whose graceful curve the figure follows. The statue is a masterpiece of 14th century French sculpture and represents a step away from the austerity and simplicity of the Gothic style towards the more mannered style then developing.

The ivory Virgin preserved in the parish church.

A view of the imposing Palace of the Popes from the far side of the river.

PLAN OF THE PALACE OF THE POPES

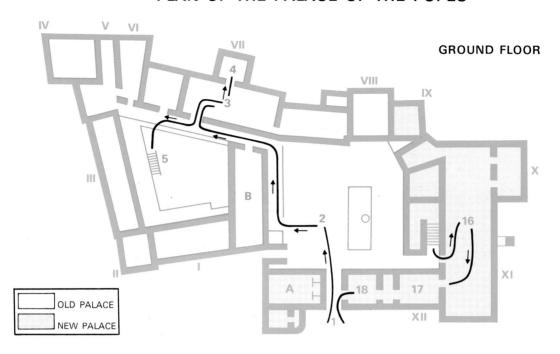

GROUND FLOOR

OLD PALACE
NEW PALACE

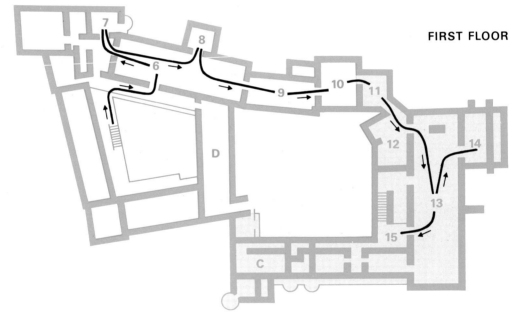

FIRST FLOOR

ROOMS IN ORDER OF VISIT

1. PORTE DES CHAMPEAUX
2. COUR D'HONNEUR
3. HALL OF THE CONSISTORY
4. CHAPELLE SAINT-JEAN
5. CLOITRE DE BENOIT XII
6. GRAND TINEL
7. UPPER KITCHEN
8. CHAPELLE SAINT-MARTIAL
9. ANTECHAMBER
10. POPE'S BEDCHAMBER
11. DEER ROOM
12. NORTH SACRISTY
13. GRANDE CHAPELLE
14. SOUTH SACRISTY
15. PORTE DE LA GRANDE CHAPELLE
     FENETRE DE L'INDULGENCE
16. SALLE DE LA GRANDE AUDIENCE
17. SALLE DE LA PETITE AUDIENCE
18. CORPS DE GARDE

CONVENTION HALLS

A - SALLE DES GARDES
B - SALLE DU CONCLAVE
C - GRAND CELLIER DE BENOIT XII
D - CHAMBRE DU TRESORIER

I - AILE DES FAMILIERS
II - TOUR DE LA CAMPANE
III - AILE DE LA CHAPELLE DE BENOIT XII
IV - TOUR DES TROUILLES
V - TOUR DE LA GLACIERE
VI - TOUR DES CUISINES
VII - TOUR SAINT-JEAN
VIII - TOUR DES ANGES
IX - TOUR DE LA GARDE-ROBE
X - TOUR SAINT-LAURENT
XI - AILE DE L'AUDIENCE
XII - TOUR DE LA GACHE